We often cannot see them, but bugs live all around us. Everywhere, billions of insects are building their homes, hunting and looking for food. They are laying eggs and protecting and feeding their young, and they are running – or flying – away from bigger animals that want to eat them.

Insects are very small animals with six legs. They have a body in three main parts:

1. **Head**
2. **Thorax**
3. **Abdomen**

six legs

Many insects can fly.

Animals that hunt and eat other animals are called predators.

Insects have two antennae (/antenie/) on their heads. These are for feeling and smelling.

antenna

wing

An insect has no bones. Instead its body has a hard outer shell called an exoskeleton (/**ex**ɑskeleten/).

Fleas are insects that live on other animals. They often live on our pet cats and dogs. They live in the fur of the animals, and use their sharp mouthparts to bite and then suck the blood (/blud/) from the animals.

cat flea

mouthparts

When a flea is filled with blood, it hops off the cat or dog. Then it lives in the carpet or in the pet's bed until it feels hungry again. When it is hungry, the flea jumps back onto the cat or dog.

A flea has extremely strong back legs, which help it to jump huge distances.

cat flea

cat fur

back legs

A colony of weaver ants makes its home from leaves. To get started, some of the weaver ants line up on the side of a leaf. Next, they grab another leaf and drag it close to the first one. Then the ants use silk to stitch the two leaves together.

weaver ant

silk stitches

larva

ant

The silk is made by young ants called larvae (/**lar**vee/). An adult ant holds one of the colony's larvae to the side of a leaf. Then the little larva makes the silk from its head.

weaver ant nest

The weaver ants keep on stitching leaves together until they have made a nest that hangs in a tree.

Leafcutter ants do not build their homes with leaves. Instead, they use leaves to grow their food. A team of leafcutter ants goes out into the forest. The ants cut small bits from leaves with their saw-like mouthparts and then carry the bits of leaf back to a fungus garden in their underground nest.

leafcutter ant

Just like little farmers, the ants feed the leaves to the fungus to make it grow. Then the ants and their young eat the fungus.

fungus garden

If you have ever seen bread with green or blue spots on it, you have seen some fungus growing. In the ants' fungus garden, the fungus grows in the same way, by feeding on the leaves.

The assassin bug is a hunter that eats ants, bees and other insects. Then it makes a gruesome backpack from the empty shells of the dead bugs!

The assassin bug uses a stabbing mouthpart to inject poison into an ant or other insect. The poison turns the insides of the ant to liquid. Then the assassin bug slurps up its slushy meal with its straw-like mouthpart.

When the ant's body is sucked dry, the assassin bug puts the empty shell on its back.

Why does the assassin bug carry dead ants on its back? One possibility is that it is trying to protect itself. If a predator were to bite the bug, it would only get a mouthful of crunchy shells!

The bee killer is a type of insect that hunts for bees. When it is time to lay her eggs, a mother bee killer digs an underground nest of little tunnels. She lays an egg in each tunnel; then she flies to a flower and waits…

a bee killer

underground nest

bee killer waiting on a flower

When a bee comes to the flower, the bee killer stings it. Then she takes the bee back to her nest and puts it next to an egg. The bee is not dead; it is just paralysed.

The bee killer goes hunting and catches a bee for each of her eggs. When the larvae hatch, each one has a meal of a fresh bee to feast on.

Dung beetles also get a first meal ready for their young. The dung beetle parents meet up at a pile of dung (poo). Together, they form a lump of the dung into a ball.

dung ball

dung beetle

Fresh dung contains lots of liquid. Many types of adult dung beetle feed on this liquid and on solid dung.

Next, the beetles dig a hole in the ground. They put the dung ball into the hole, and the mother beetle lays an egg inside the poo. When the larva hatches from its egg, it is inside a ball of yummy dung that it can eat!

larva

dung ball

The larva of a scarlet lily beetle does not eat poo, but it does use it as a disguise! When a lily beetle larva hatches from its egg, it feeds on leaves — lots of leaves. All that eating, means that the larva makes lots of poo, which it sticks to its body.

adult scarlet lily beetle

scarlet lily beetle larva

The plump larva does this to protect itself from birds and other predators that want to eat it. The clever poo disguise makes the larva look like a sticky, brown bird dropping!

a larva inside its poo disguise

The looper moth caterpillar is another insect with a clever disguise. It looks just like a twig!

When a bird or other predator gets close, the caterpillar stays very still. It can even hold onto a twig with its legs and make its body stand upright. Any predators are fooled into thinking that it is a twig, and not a caterpillar at all.

twig

looper moth caterpillar

legs

When an animal makes itself look like something else, it is called mimicry.